Night Manual

Night
Manual

Poems by David Hornibrook

Wayne State University Press
Detroit

MADE IN MICHIGAN WRITERS SERIES

General Editors
Michael Delp, Interlochen Center for the Arts
M. L. Liebler, Wayne State University

ISBN 978-0-8143-4662-4 (paperback); ISBN 978-0-8143-4663-1 (e-book)

Library of Congress Control Number: 2018963208

Publication of this book was made possible by a generous gift from The Meijer Foundation. This work is supported in part by an award from the Michigan Council for Arts and Cultural Affairs.

Wayne State University Press
Leonard N. Simons Building
4809 Woodward Avenue
Detroit, Michigan 48201-1309

Visit us online at wsupress.wayne.edu

They are bewildered by the land;
the wilderness has closed them in.

—Exodus 14:3

Contents

ONE

Before August

Death was a theory. Wind was wind. I took a walk & wrote a poem about the light *glancing off mirrored leaves*. It was a bad poem. The light was *luminous*.

Back then the silver maple behind our house—a *mere* tree. Evenings were filled with names. This was before animals could speak. She was unusually tired but took time to plant marigolds. I bought a box of chocolate cigars.

The stars were fixed like earth, stable. Wine still tasted good. Greenish tomatoes lay wrapped in newspaper in the kitchen. I took one in my hand, added it to another. I said I had two, not three.

First Light

She sounds like cobblestone when she sleeps,
but wakes early, before the grass, the burning
bushes or tiger lilies; only the roots of our
willow are awake at this hour breathing,
stretching in the loamy darkness. And the skunk
in the garden, how quietly it paws the moist soil,
grazing for crickets. In the kitchen's dim light,
she pours coffee into her favorite mug. She settles
deeply into the green armchair with her Bible
the color of oak leaves worn by the sun.
On an August morning in Michigan my mother
adjusts her large glasses and reads. She reads
as though the small print were clusters of tiny
criminals she must keep from escaping
into the bright world.

Versions of a Summer

1

Mornings after rain, the pools on the sidewalk
shimmer. Some days   are perfect for walking, other

days, I know the knives are close behind.

2

Deer rip the flame-licked sunflowers from their stalks
and eat them whole.   Once, I watched a pale tomato worm

burrow into the green fruit.

3

When the water is cloudy, the swimmers
think twice.   Sometimes, when I'm not watching,

the plecostomus comes out of hiding.

4

How did I fail to realize the heads on Easter Island were giants
buried to the neck?   At the Gentleman's Green

no one turns the sprinklers off when it rains.

5

At noon—I have perfected the art of nervous laughter, climbing
out of someone else's   swimming pool,

dripping and searching for a towel.

6

I watch the blue heron glide over the pond, I watch the night heron
shift on its branch.

I watch the cars go by on the road.

7

Nights when summer reaches its most terrible heat

the beads of sweat on the air conditioner start to evaporate, the machine

groans and threatens to evict me.

8

In my dream, all the bodies in the world made one
body.   A fierce, five-headed body

splashed with paint and fire.

9

Van Morrison sings Tupelo Honey in 1971 and I'm hearing it
decades later   over wall-mounted speakers in a coffee shop.

It's common now, to see hawks drifting over the road.

Preservation

On a Tuesday, I leave work early & drive to a small gravel parking
      lot beyond which St. John's Marsh stretches

into pale distance. A single star hangs
              low in the sky. I emerge

from the car & walk the circumference of the marsh, pausing
      as a heron strikes

the nearby water & rises, bluegill in beak. The bird stands motionless
          a moment, before swallowing.

Further along the path, a turtle topples off the edge of a log
      & vanishes beneath the water.

A day moon appears in the bright sky & the star, probably
        a passing airplane, is gone.

I climb down through sedges, toward the water's edge, accidentally
      startling a bass. Mud blooms

in the water as the fish plunges from sight. Early this morning, I read
        about rogue black holes roaming

the universe. Super-massive
      & unhinged, they consume

everything in their horizon: planets, moons, even
      stars.

Don't worry, read the article, *no cause for concern, these events are*
      rare and the universe vast.

Pax Americana

Music swept
through an apartment window & became lost

in traffic. Beyond the complex, simple hills burned
all day. Sunlight

rode the curve of a ringlet straight
into my glance. Dangerous birds

flocked. The smoking
bride on the hill above the boardwalk

said: *it's time to leave.* Meanwhile, the sun

singed the tips of the grass, swollen green
apples hung

in the trees, & the sky sucked

water from small puddles
in the parking lots. In those days a dog

roamed the neighborhood. We learned
to tell time by way of warning.

Divers often emerged from the river bearing
brass rings of old keys. Every hour

there was a test of the emergency broadcast system.
Often, cats gathered beneath the window to listen.

Separation

Though no one   *said*

the root was dying
said the   *first light*

was   *dawning*
in the hills

no one said   *hills*

one was not laid on top of another

there was no cockcrow no*mount* or *mound*
nothing was   *fixed*

no moon
no lingering star

a wetness was not   *laid upon the grass*

there was no last   *cleaving*

no rain   *blending*
the hours

THE CHINESE FARMER SELLS HIS ROBOTS

—Later, I began to call them my sons

I didn't sleep for days after selling the child,
made by man in man's image a secondhand
      image of God like the sun
glancing off polished sheet metal.

Born of gears
inside a daydream of that *marvelous human motion,*
      sweetly green curvatures of wire.

Freshly oiled cogs turning
day to twilight delicately
the way a hair bends, he could bend
      and bow.

Harvest moon,
      a little Autumn rain.
Beautiful Wu, a simple
      mind unfolded in lovely form.

Apollo on the Block

The god on his bike rode to warn us:
a swerve of wind would bring the house down.

So what if the people scatter,
if the wind-up rooster cracks a spring,

the neighborhood was bound to change
and the child was bound to lose what he would.

Tonight is the night the family gathers at the brick stove
to watch the leaves burn, tonight is the night

the god on his bike
pops the last wheelie.

Nocturne

i

The doe springs lightly into the trap.   Stars click
against glass,   night

slips through a gap   in the window.

The edge comes to graze the white   plain, the warm
forest waits.

ii

Lush beasts tangle in the grass after
dark. A soft

vowel mounts a whisper and rides up
against the teeth of a hard   consonant. Two sounds

tumble into a single   word. Planetary

iii

bodies, each

with its own circling moon, blend gravities.
Unclasped,   the hills of one

plumb the lakes of the other
until one more
flashing apocalypse

in a long history of worlds breaking   apart. Sheared

off,   continents cascade

into space.

THE ULTRASOUND

What does it matter life
      in other galaxies. Even the moon

gathers what it
      loves but never close enough.

It is cold. My tired
      wife does not want

to read magazines.
      I wonder what it's like

to halo yourself around
      something nameless.

In *Discover,* I read
      about holes so deep

that nothing, even
      light, can escape. Say a star

enters & we
      theorize about where it goes.

We go where the nurse leads us

& I don't
      remember when I first

learned about gravity.
      My wife lies down on a bed

& lifts her shirt up
		just below her breasts.

A woman spreads gel
		across the planet.

My eyes are pulled to the monitor

where a universe expands
		or contracts, I can't tell which.

Turbulence within a cloud
		of space dust will cause a knot

to form, the dust around it
		collapsing. Is it motion

the monitor reveals
		or just the wand

brooding over the face
		of the waters? The hot core

at the heart of a collapsing cloud
		will one day become a star.

After a while everyone leaves us alone.

Later, one woman
		returns. Her gaze attends

the space around us. She asks
		for us to step into the hallway.

We don't know how to get there.

Some Instructions

Paste winter over this last week of August.
Strip the wavering leaves, douse

branches black. Cold powder
the lawn. Cap the juniper

in white. Turn the rosebush
into a network

of thorns
thinly cased in ice.

Stand under the silver maple
where the sun itself makes silvery

the rivers sluicing down
the trunk.

Forget what you know about
about summer.

Let the cold come.

Gone

In late mid-morning
      walking the causeway across St. John's
Marsh not entirely without
      hope I came
to search in the fog.

You said
      you must be going you
red-winged blackbird
      flicking from reed to tree
& back to reed

& that was that.
      ——

Your voice a small
      wetland flower
grown over by
      reeds whose
weedy stalks choke out
      the sedges. Soon
there will be no
      food for mallards,
black, wood or crested
      ducks. As I walked
I heard
      loon laughter. You,

a slender
       shield fern
in shade from a crop
       of black willow.
Tree swallows
       flapped in the buttonbush, over
wild leeks
       & arrowhead with their
tiny white
       breathy blossoms.

       ——

You everywhere I looked
blazoned the bottom of raindrops
woven into cumulonimbus hundreds
of feet in the air.

       ——

You were gone,
       your name.

In my dream I was Great
Heron chasing
       across moist sky,

I dipped
       & ran smack
into God stepping
on the carcass
              of a massasauga rattler.

       ——

your voice is cool
water rolling off the turtles' backs

———

Where did the fog go, where are
the American toads? Their sound
left, silent as mushrooms
growing on fallen logs.

I catch a glimpse of your navy
skirt turning into the distance
over twenty years.

> *Indian Grass is gone, Big Blue Stem too*
> *Blazing star & Tall*
> *Sunflower nowhere*
> *It's so dry,*
> *dry.*

———

I would arrive before you, pluck all
the wild blueberries surrounded
by green marsh water, enshrined
by the sounds of blackbirds
those sweet berries, I would hand
you a bowl, watch you eat.

———

In my dream
you had begun to sing
though I could
no longer see or touch you
      sang

    ——

God a song,
now?
      Like God,
to answer with a question.
      A fox slipped from behind
      bramble & flashed
across the path. A faint smell
of distant lightning. Water
poured
      from a stone, so
          I drank deep

AUBADE

In this place where deer have spent   the night

the grass lies down like hair across   a bed

circled by slender grass laced   with violets
surrounded by   a density

of maple black locust and oak

a hawk swings in   a drowsy
oval over the   clearing

and squirrels leap   from one limb
to another

a small infinity unfolded in   the wilderness

a short time later a boy

playing an old guitar crosses the edge

of the field & disappears into   the wood

Two

A Stand of Pine

The sweetest apples hung
highest in the tree. I broke
every branch trying to
reach one. Five minutes
after eating it, I no longer knew
what it tasted like. Everything goes—
every single smooth, oblong
rock from my collection, every
pitted, banded gem—Petoskey
stones, geode crystals, fool's gold.
Also the record covers I pinned
to the wall. Also, the whole garbage
bag of 8-tracks. So much
John Denver no one will ever
hear. So much Marianne Faithful
surrendered to tape rot.
So much hiss & scramble falling
out of the world. Also
the Monster In My Pockets: Jutland
Troll, Huron the Hunter, Wendigo,
Red Cap, Manticore, Beast—
they all crept away like stories
clipped from skateboard magazines,
superhero trading cards lost
for weeks then found neatly
stacked on the desktop. But even

desktop is nowhere now.
So much slippage along the river's
edge—land constantly giving way
to motion. The sinkhole down
the street that swallowed a truck
& the mounds of dirt as big
as houses we climbed to get
a better look. What could
be done with so much earth, where
could it possibly have gone?

After August

The wind grew a tongue
& spoke

through trees. A cricket
leapt into the burning bush.

The fountain collapsed. Daylight, a broken
fish, followed

night. A death song
broke on the kitchen floor.

The backyard sky split
in half

by the flight of ducks. We opened
a bottle

as if our hands, abrupt
ends,

could only grind like stones

as if the sun had failed. The earth
a hawk

suddenly cold.

Shadow Country

[1]

We played with dandelions:

mama had a baby & her head popped off.

[2]

Once upon a time we took apart
the nest to build a house.

We framed a photograph
of the moon above
the fireplace, called

the house home.

[3]

A world made in darkness.

What was she, this world
with her paper fingernails?

What was he, this world
with his *form & void*?

[4]

Once upon a time the key
felt good in hand, a ripe
fruit. Where did it go?

Did she toss it into the well?
When will I understand it was not well?

[5]

If we believe flames are holy, why not
build a pile of dry sticks in the kitchen?

[6]

Why is there a *man* in the moon?
Is there fire on the surface? I heard
that oceans breathe inside that stone

(couldn't he drown?) which lays
light down over the place we build
& rebuild our house, where we
house our coffee mugs & all
the names.

[7]

Let's plant a pine
in the floor, watch
it grow, build a nest

in the branches, rub
dandelions into our
skin until we're

yellow, paste
feathers to our arms
and pretend
we are eggless,
      flightless
birds screeching &
      leaping from the nest
flailing our false
wings & our darker
      real wings our wild
shadow-maker
      wings over this dim
          indistinguishable country.

Translations

It's true.

I was careful.

The lines I made were clean.

She can't deny her shadow fell from her like silk.

My own fell upwards, taken by warm radiator breeze.

We blessed the knife, placed it under the bed.

We were thirsty then.

I said the water from this faucet tastes hard.

She said there cannot be water inside of a stone.

I said there is nothing sadder than milk.

She said she preferred non-pasteurized, non-homogenized.

I said there is no color like orange.

She said the oranges on the desk are no longer good.

I said that ice was found on the moon.

She said there was ice in the freezer.

I said I wanted to go to sleep.

She said fine.

SIGNS

The morning after   we

thought there was a word for
        last night

rain cast itself lightly into pools

we played chess with our body
        language

such clockish & baroque motions

later on
        water spilled over the gutters

do you remember the words   we used
        to mean

right now I think of you while I cross

the arcade & witness a woman
        touch

a man's lips with a single
        finger

not your body is next to me

I don't understand how to call this
        my hand

reaching through space

DURING THE NIGHT

The agents of rain
came down to investigate
the branches of our maple. I can't say
what they found with their silver
brushes. All I know

is that the bodies
of the grass bore down and let hours
of darkness and wind sweep over
them. They were, all
of them, monks.

I wanted her
to wake up and loose
birds from her quilt. I wanted
the storm to charge over our house,
floods to spill, things to burn.

Instead, this patient
investigation. This soft-fingered
questioning. She rolled over
and smiled the rain continued.

WEATHER

I'm travelling forty miles an hour on a bus with a brown bag of apples from the food co-op. I imagine the smile on her face when she sees this clean organic fruit.

Tinsel drops of rain tap the glass and rivers roll down the windows. Perhaps she will cut out the cores and stuff the apples with butter and cinnamon

and the entire house will smell like cinnamon!

But what if this is the wrong bus
and I'm already late—she may be in bed by now. What if these apples, grown free
from soil without pesticide or gene splice are spotty

and overripe?

It's been raining since early this morning and our garden I imagine
is flooded—smaller plants washed away and waterlogged cucumbers
floating in a muddy pond, the stems of bean plants broken.

Clouds anchor the sky to the west. Turning onto Lancaster Avenue, where a group
of strangers hold black umbrellas and wait beside the road, it's possible this bus

is already years late.

INSOMNIA

And the posts of the door moved
at the voice of him that cried, and
the house was filled with smoke

                        —Isaiah 6:3–4

This night
an oily
tide licks
the empty
beach. No
use, the chalk
of an extinguished
coal
pressed
to lip. A doused
flame blacks
the water. No one
on earth
tonight. One
dread leaf glides
back & forth
in the slow wind
& does not
fall.

CONFESSION

Bees hum everywhere in the apple orchard. I'm tired of October, where everywhere the hum of bees in the pumpkin patch, leaves blow all over the city, the bees circle. A pumpkin full of bees lies in a field and fields of bees blow through the streets. Even the church buzzes with their chant. Rumor says the priests of the bees have already flown off with the children. Nowhere is safe, even the confessionals: makeshift hives. Please, come find me. I have stolen the honey; I have taken a sweetness I can no longer taste.

A Poem after Anger

The god scoured the neighborhood
left a trail of cast-off bodies in its wake

his skin felt   *appropriate*
smelled electric like scorched coffee

left burn marks & broken
branches   the god is still young

& knows the feel of wings
thinks *listen*   is something to do

with hands
like shaking a tree until the fruit falls

the apple that fell here
turned to soil

so we dug up the seeds &
let the wind take them away

a kicked can of paint left
a permanent gash

of *heritage red* on the driveway
let this be a sign

next time
may the god pass over us

October, Late Afternoon

Since the child from the neighborhood went missing, I can't keep

from tripping over every toy
        my own children leave

on the stairs. Summer in shadow.
        No matter what happens, it will be

night soon & judging

by the veil's thickness, the stars
        will be invisible. I stand in the back

yard, feel every motion the wind
        plays across my face. The only One

I love has a body
        made of questions, but I was taught to be afraid

to ask. A snake tongue flickering
        in space. King Solomon

dreaming in the weeds. It shall be
        given to you. I try

to take God's name in vain. Instead, I sing
        the names

of every one
        I love, this woman, these children, over

& over, ashes
        & ashes, & fall.

King's Crossing

I see a house that is breaking
down   a father
                    in a basement mixing
chemicals by lamplight

        Two birds connected by string

in a field   adjacent to the house   adjacent to a forest

a mother lays one dogwood
                                    leaf on top of a maple leaf
inside the forest is a cave
and a stone
            dressed in moss
                        a lost cat with magic

power and outside the forest money flies

from the house like a flock
                            of hummingbirds dripping
        honey colored
                    fire on the lawn

only a white flag tied to a green   branch sings

the children
                spread frosting on a beautiful cake

while below ground

                the man

tries

      to decipher a language that doesn't

exist

      inside the house

is a table that   is the river rising

      inside the house   is a clock that is

a moon   that does not keep

DIRE COUNTRY

Wallpaper of wild geese caught
mid-flight on the doctor's office wall.

Here among magazines, in a room folded away from the sun,
I'm waiting to be nested in labels,

to be slivered & collected, clipped to a board in small
print, puzzled, pieced
                             & fraught, waiting for the doors to swing
open for a stranger
to call my name.

It's hard to stay safe.

In between soap operas, on the waiting room television—lawyers
         lucking up money. *We'll make them pay!*

& the miracle drugs promise to save you
                                    from an eternity of restless legs.

Who will drain
         blood from the lungs?   Who knew death hid inside tomato soup cans

& lapped
around the microwave, quickening circuits?

The heaving, surging horse of death & its drowsy stall.
Once, I was afraid aliens

would suck me out of the shower, straight through the ceiling.

Could even our own
house be safe? And now, my wife says

it lives in the phone in my pocket, in the black box
blinking in the basement, sending out ever widening circles,

penetrating us in our sleep. *We're killing our children*, she says,

but all I know
is that it's been hours, wilderness   & still   geese.

THREE

Motion & Eclipse

If not for the supermoon blooming over Michigan
in the fall of that year the intoxicated man would
not have approached us passing by the theatre.

Blame it on the rain, for example, dripping from
awnings long after the storm was over. Particular
forces. Wing thrusts for example, propelling the goose

beyond reach of the fox. Cosmic dramas enacted on
small bodies, ours included—all physics and physical,
a dropped bottle splintering into shards upon striking,

for example, pavement. The geese gather in the park
to prepare for long migration. We walk our six blocks
in the direction of a particular bench where we will

sit together and look at the moon. Cars pass
in both directions. We are not the only ones walking
on this street but we choose to decide the meaning

of our touch. Slivers of the visible universe reflect
everywhere in still puddles. Crisp air blows evenly
from left to right. Intent thrives in our warm

equations. The man was not intentional. He failed
at choosing though he was harmless, just drunk.
The early humans crossed a bridge made of land

to get to this place. Then the earth moved
and the world became new. Still, no one called it
a *New World* until it was already very old and then

only by ignorance, perhaps intentional. Eventually
the man wandered off muttering to himself. Leftover
rain left the ground shiny and a little slick. We fail

to consider that *we* are the ones flying through space.
By imperceptible movements an earth tide shifted
the sidewalk twelve inches closer to the sky.

It was late October. When you pulled me
close to your body it had nothing
to do with sexual love. The geese

were never metaphors for how to leave
behind. They were only ever birds
crossing in front of the moon.

Prayer

I come in early
take off my

coat boil
water for tea

roast beef &
muenster on

grilled rye
for lunch

wash the last
few dishes

in the sink
outside no

wind in
the cold

orchard the
air bears

a chill
not a single

leaf
clings

Amen

TRANSGRESSION

When the ice was thick enough
I walked out onto the lake

was she out there smoking a cigarette
in all that night

if so we didn't
speak to each other

but together stared up into the darkness
at all the trespassing light

rising off the city like heat
& above us stars

afraid to leave the safety of their caves

After the Party I Will Walk Alone into Snow-Covered Hills

I will myself become a hill & all night
be still & remember things

a hill would remember & sit
the way a hill would sit

under a mass of stars

I will know the tongue a hill
speaks the names of trees emerging

from the arched back of a hill the way
it feels for a hill to sleep

of course a hill does not
sleep so I will dream

awake in the cold
night & the warmer day

& know well
the slope of my life

I will go become a hill
& wear easily the grass

& without complaint the coat
of snow come

looking for me & I will feel
the pressure of your steps

feel free to lie down & see

what there is of stars
& night—but not yet

the party isn't
over—the guests just now

knocking at the door

Trickster August

Long after he left my radar, he came over the radio. I could hear him
un-crinkling behind the music.

Later, his shadow passed between lines of a poem I was reading
so I closed the book and went for a walk.

Maybe he was wedged into the cracks in the sidewalk. Before long

he was definitely on television, lurking
in the breath of the weatherman, spread over the microphone

of the American Idol. Then, in the pork
chop I glazed with ranch, in the shadow my hand and fork

cast over the dinner table. Soon, I was certain I saw him
sitting in my favorite chair, drinking my coffee. Then

outside, he was staring from the apple tree's leafless branch.

One wet, cold morning I felt his tiny voice
crawl across my forehead.

I went to the doctor because there must be a cure for this,
but as soon as I said that, I knew

he was in the medicine.

I became enamored with the length of needles.
The stethoscope was scary.

He burrowed into my ears. I could hear his desires, the thick quiet milk of his thoughts. He began whispering.

He was as real as black ice on the way home from the hospital.

Don't ever tell me he didn't exist.
You don't exist.

Event Horizon

The   garage   is
kept   warm   by
kerosene   and   ire.
There   is   a   box   of
bolts,   a   box   of
screws   and   nuts
&   clamps
&   saws
&   planes
& everything
that   cuts,   holds,
smoothes
&   fixes what
it makes.   In
outer space

●

begins   to   drift
across some portion
of the universe. The
first star gripped by
that   nothing   folds
into   itself   like   a
father
and vanishes.

Evening Comes

Quiet layers of snow at the bottom
of the sea. Someone pulls a trash can

to the curb. Barely a hum & all down the street
the lights blink on. Inside, we prepare to leave

for the city—clothes on, shoes tied, backpack full
of medicine. The moths brush against

the door their ghostly
wings & we walk outside

together. We get into the car.

You've come to conjure the same dream
again, a neural trench worn into your nights

& the bright buildings of the city rise
as we near them like terrible stones dredged

from beneath the snow of that dream.

The boat goes dark
under wave. A cold cup filled

with rain. You aren't thirsty but still
drink the glass empty.

The empty glass drinks us both.

Damn Good Living

Where you go I will go, and where you stay
I will stay. Your people will be my people

—Ruth 1:16

[*you're safe here   it's ok   you're safe here*   ]

✳

buzzer sounds and a guard presses open the heavy double doors

✳

enter endless corridor

✳

windowless

✳

a picture in a long hallway of evening sun lighting up a field of flower-
ing trees & shockingly green grass

✳

[*I'm your friend   of course   I won't leave you   of course*   ]

✳

the color sucks into a single saturated rectangle.

✳

leave as soon | as possible | as papers are signed | as door closes

✳

[*nothing to worry about   the people here just want   to talk   nothing*

    to worry   to talk   about to worry   just

    worry   talk   just talk]

✻

this afternoon the rain fell steadily

✻

[*Let's get in the car   Let's go for a ride   Let's go*]

✻

humidity soaked evening light
leaves & grass tinged with a green somehow

✻

richest palette of dark gray & blue bled together in the sky above
disappearing city

✻

| *I am a citizen* | *I am a citizen* | *I'm not a citizen* | *I'm a citizen* |

PONY

When I finally left the man alone with the doctors and tried to get back home
to where my family was likely just sitting down to dinner, & wandered

through the subterranean passages of the hospital where exposed
pipes were veins connecting the walls to the workings of this beast

whose hunger for the meat of people sounded like metal salt falling,
I couldn't do it. Echoes of footsteps rung in the chambers, the janitor

in the distance was a faceless, helpless thing. I lost my body inside
the shiny bones of a pony, I couldn't find

the right doorway or my fingers, the right set of stairs or some
familiar hand to lead me to the well-lit reception area, the glass

doors and their covenant. No directions printed
on the cavern walls. No linear paint on the floor. Everything

wet, discolored moss. I galloped through the tunnels
after a flicker of light, some distant memory of pasture.

Pop Blasted

1

We were all interested in the future. Suddenly we were looking in clean rooms for
art. Especially in California, especially between Hindu temples & launch pads.
Always in search of the post-sputnik deep & lasting, wandering through Wayne
McAllister's curvaceous hotels for something smaller and usually less direct
than the dominant visual language of motels, it was sometimes called Googie,
after Lautner's design, after the coffee shop, the Chemosphere, after all, we are all
astronauts. Space-age bachelor-
pad music? The ice-

white cube?

2

The celebrity psychic Criswell at the beginning of the 1959 astro-disaster had a
perfect way to explain the influence of the saucer men's standard kind of ascetic
interior. Cities & highways, as if seen anew from space, upswept. Capsule-
shaped living devices seemed to evoke far-out geodesic spirits. We may not have
been thinking about tubular & machinelike, about silvery streamlining, though
certainly architects, said Richard Rogers, we could draw parallels—satellite shape
& starburst. There were unconscious threads as well—suits expanding & doubling
as structures. Black & white severed alien hand wreaking havoc on the outskirts of
town.

> Greetings, my friend, from infancy,
>   for that

>   is where you & and I are headed.

PARABLE

A man emerged from the woods dragging a box that was too heavy for him. He left it lying in a field and spent the rest of the evening at Edgar's reading captions on old black & white movies across the bar. When he'd had enough, he went home, took off his coat & sweater, took off his shoes & socks, closed the living room curtains, drank a glass of water, went upstairs to bed and let himself be lulled to sleep by the sound of the fish tank and the monstrous droning.

PSALM

It is written that you remember we are dust

You inhaled deeply

In the steady rush
of your exhale we began dreaming

That was a long time ago

There were days you saw fit
we found solace in the taste of ash

From where we stand here now in the night
even your love looks like the city on fire

Let us believe you again
here on the snow-crusted land

& listen to the timbre
of your voice in the pines

Or else may we uncover a window
in the burning house

Self Portrait w/ Wrecking Ball

[1]

In 2013, there is no door. The church is locked from the inside.
The other church is on fire & I have a body.

> What is this for, this hand?
> Slow entrance? Touching the face?

> And this mouth?
> This art of naming animals?

And you, love, where is your finger ring?

[2]

Facebook keeps showing Miley with her mouth open.
& I keep finding little things wrong   with everything.

> In the museum of WTF, the art of grease smeared across
> glass. The seer's tongue is only one piece on display.

A resurrection too, for reals. Sleeping inside a coffin to confuse the faithful.
A curious picture of a mirror and a face with doors with windows in the doors.

> A wax figure of a woman breaking bricks out of a wall. A framed
question:

> what?

Exhibit #324

> The willow tree was not real.

> [if there was anything I wanted
> it was for the willow to be real]

[3]

Says TV preacher: *plant a small seed*! Says

old Steppenwolf Greatest Hits record
spinning in the living room: *your wall's too high.* Says

        Starbucks: *coffee speaks to you.*   Says I: *no.*
Says daughter: *I want your scratchy face.*

Says cat: there is no cat here, says
doctor: *do you smoke*? Says

        Linda: *come home early*? Says

God:

Says Miley: *let me in.*

Says God:

[4]

        Says Miley: *you wreck me.*

Says news radio: *there's going to be a negotiation here.*

        Says Billy Graham: *the most eloquent prayer is the prayer through hands.*

Says wild mazes chalked
          across the driveway: *here is everything you need to know.*

Says I: *you,* and   *also you.*

[5]

This morning

a hawk corkscrewed its body from the top
of the neighbor's cottonwood

and narrowly missed
its prey,   lucky starling.
              This evening

                        I am a hundred miles away
                  walking past downtown to a friend's

small apartment
for Monday dinner.
          Last night

              I dreamed I climbed willow branches into some ruin, some
              church, was sorting through smashed concrete for little

              shards of glass. Miniature complicated crucifixes
              appeared. I couldn't collect them all and people I love were

              watching from the windows.

Last night, I dreamed & finally everything burned away.
There was just the one thing,
                  that one

                      clear thing.

Tonight I will dream   again
to find out what a body has to do.

FOUR

VESPERS

In this dark garden
I shave the hair
from my head

This evening
the body finds itself alone
in the lights vanishing

& the Beloved unwraps
a parcel of silence

In this dark garden
words come
to recover their bodies

This evening
the day's shadows
wash in deeper shades

& holy thunder
whispers among the trees

In this dark garden
I walk with
the Friend

This evening
my eyes light on the path
lonely & sleep descends

on a soft storm of light
oh soft Storm of Light

In this dark garden
my ears receive
the song of the Beloved

& the Beloved lights
the lamp of the moon

TIDES

gaze through
longing like a telescope
     things far appear

close

     doe running
nearby
     across distant
hillside

✯

top drawer
of my father's
dresser his stainless
steel spyglass

we stared at the moon
in January
the size of a quarter
it smelled like snow

✯

another January
a different *we*

made bricks
of snow

with a shovel & cardboard box
the kids played on the wall
all day until their cheeks burnt red

✳

if you go far
enough into the cold
deep enough
into the glass
alone enough
into the eye
through
the insatiable ring
you emerge
near Lake Michigan
near the end
of summer

✳

this time waves
  lap August
    back to shore she

  is light blue hardly
      the furthest end

          of an echo

✳

further a little
        further   & eggshell sand
                        laughter & gulls coasting
the long thigh of the beach
white arcs trace
           the seven-month sphere emerging   from water

the moon   within which we have   determined   is August
                ✳

           moon pulls
    anything on earth
to bring it closer
    but earth holds on
to everything
        but water   impossible shape

you can depend on water
           who can hold
             cannot be held
embodied mystery
        pulled moonward
earthward
from this gentle
     tug of war
comes sound
     motion whatever
is essential & unable
       to be spoken

＊

Job sat for days
scraping his boils
his wife asked—
why not curse
God & die

he told her
she spoke as one
of the foolish women

had one of his three
friends given Job a glass
peering into it he would
have seen

      her wisdom
            their children   snow

               in January

＊

spring now
staring through ground glass
at a hillside leftover
spruce cones gleam
on the grass

rain is silent mist remains
a mistake to imagine
maybe no one else is alive

Time Lapse

Near the top of the hill a doe
crosses the field of vision
toward clustered walnut trees

———

Portentous clouds
thin leaving

     blue

———

Canada geese
scissor the

     sky despite

appearances
does not sever

STILL

It is not
     a tangle

of petals
     in the rain

a blossom
     of hands

a name does
     not sprout

from the
     vines of it.

COMPLINE

Together in the spilled wine's miniature lake
      we prayed, but knew a wilderness, and homeless, our words
          grew feral.

In her infinite plainness
I have known her, called her
              wife, even her name
                    mouthed into eyes. My own
                       dropped into dark pools.

     In water, we mingled
              in the trouble.

There was a task:
      a little street through the wood,
      tongues in the trees, no one
      to keep the temple burning, unless . . .

Neither of us read the instructions
printed on the skin, under eyelids, behind
earlobes, no. There was nothing

written there. How could we
              know? All night instead, and each night
    this holding
          must continue, this
               speaking, this silence.

We count the passing months.

Something small
       tattooed to the moon's skin. A pity
          we couldn't name the child.
          And then we did.

AUGUST

Gravity cracks the egg,
keeps things   in motion,

yolk slides   across
        the white linoleum.   Step
and step.

        Your body
follows mine
                this evening,   new
from other evenings

Otis Redding
                sings,   Ray Charles
sings, outside
                the rain   sings.

Your leg, a robin
                bedding down   among
the apple blossoms,
descends.   I move—
                brittle pine.
The floor needs
mopping,   tender
        as an eggshell your
fingernail grazes
                skin of my forearm.

Where is it

         written? Look there,

tease out

       the two   children, clean

    kitchen,

a dozen smooth   eggs

         white

    and cold

minus one.

        She had skin

the texture of a hydrangea petal.

Letter to a Friend

What time is it in the other country

at this precise moment when I am
writing this letter to you? I imagine

you drinking water from a glass bottle.

✳

You will read this letter
on a boat with white sails:

Seagulls swoop overhead. The sun
midway through the sky, the waves choppy.

Your hand passes

across your face, brushes aside
your hair, but

isn't it really my
hand, passing

your hand across
your face?

✳

Here, in this country, I'm writing
this letter, it is noon

exactly & classical
music plays over the speakers

at Starbucks. Starbuck was a sailor
too, though the coffee part

was a marketer's
dream, a fantasy

having nothing to do with these
caramel walls, loud

music, cold
conditioned air

& wobbly tables.
The coffee inside

this cup is black. It is
warm & warms
my body. I bring

the cup to my lips, set the cup
down again, finish this

letter.

WHAT IF I GREW DARK

Elderly   could mean

cured, again.   Night would not
fall & stars   would walk   slowly off

the stage. By then   you would know
the scent   of hostas, lemon

lilies. The wall   of the house
would glow

with moonflower

vines strung   like crowns,   blossoms
closing   carefully, practiced

folds, because now
the   moth

is not *lighting*   on the petals

& light   is not dawning, yet.
I will be   silent.   Waiting,

still dark,   pregnant, the cumbersome
skunk disappears   in the bushes,

a dream,   entering. What if really,
the ending,   something more

like opening.   Morning
informs the night,   its word

inscribed   in the face   of the sky.
The sound   of doves   cooing

instead of   that bald   ringing
of bells &   metaphors.

Axis Mundi

Tonight, while walking through woods back to the cabin
I strain to see the path ahead and look—   there's the bridge!

Over the bridge, last night's storm laid down
a pine. I duck underneath to cross:

what is this needled through space   & time? And somewhere
across America

five hundred thousand light bulbs burn out.

I emerge from the woods   five hundred thousand stars.

White lichen grows along the path, the ground
glows lunar

& bristles with light. I sit down   & here in the darkness begin
eating grapes from a plastic bag—they burst

between my teeth & I'm surprised
by their uncommon sweetness. I think about the   One thread through my

space & time, the pine
that grounds   the cosmic spiral fallen
across a bridge.

The night passes as I go on eating grapes. The next day
I go fishing & try to forget about the tree.

A day passes, then another
& I return, look out

& the bridge
is gone. The pine

stands dressed in sun & jeweled
with dew. Taller than I remember, it rises

above the ravine.

Night Manual

Step 1:

Let father empty his wallet. And owls & pyramids pour

into that great bath—the sea. Let water
flow from the broken
branch. The ocean used to be made of comic books & orange
juice. Let us all be California girls.

Step 2:

Wilderness
        will fold back
into your extended hand when
                                you let sugar fall over the lawn. Someone said
        space was cluttered

with junky stars. Let nice
                    boys disappear. Let Gumby remember

that Pokey is a person too. Freedom
                                    will ring, whatever
            you do, don't

answer.
        Let your eyeballs be the police.

Step 3:

Climb up the slippery willow into wet
                               fields of constellations.

Let Dr. Floyd lean back in the womb chair   and relax
before he contemplates   the meaning of
                                the monolith.
Gravity is
      a game we play. Everything is
                    a game we play. Let there be
light. Let it snow,   let it smile.

Let fires build
      until dawn, son, on this   birthday cake earth.

What I Did This Morning

Woke up, put on a T-shirt, walked downstairs and made coffee.
Broke a couple eggs while reaching into the fridge for an orange,

cleaned up, wondered if the Tigers would beat the Twins.
Went upstairs and checked on the kids: still asleep.

I covered them and went back to the kitchen.
Stared out and for a long moment

the white faces of apple blossoms, the maple
branches, curling their hands, announced a coming

rain, a heron passed in the distance, a small
dark spot on the face of the crescent

moon. Rabbits lurked in the garden. I opened
the screen, banged pots together to scare them off.

Four Songs for Missing

i

carrying clipped
   heads of marigolds
to keep away
    mosquitos
she approaches the
   land of once her
body.

ii

  rubber ball lost
under the stove

I found it last week
while replacing the element

covered in dust
hair and grease

different
for being lost
  for being found

iii

the body
  has its
little
grievances

                the hairs continue
well
into the night

                                        iv
                        the eye
                            satisfied
                        sifted from a beach
                                    of sand we call   *stars*
                        she was
                            small and growing
                        smaller   after the apple

                        blossoms had long passed on

84

LAUDS

In this quiet room
I light the candle
that burns to God

This morning words
slip the cases off their bodies
& rise from the dark

In this quiet room
I take apart
my eyes to see

This morning damp fires
mark the earth's last night
& once more the first dawn

In this quiet room
I unlace this scar
to see this ember glow inside

This morning the center
of the cross flares open
into every direction

In this quiet room
the Beloved speaks
& the body listens

Acknowledgments

Many thanks to the editors and readers of the following journals in which these poems, or versions of them, first appeared:

Orange Quarterly, Zau, Thrush Poetry Journal, Rogue Agent, SiDEKiCK LIT, Day One, Five Quarterly, Almost Five, The Columbia Review, Shark Reef, Flyway, Dunes Review, The Bear River Review, Stone's Throw Magazine, Innisfree Poetry Journal.

"The Ultrasound" was reprinted in *Pushcart Prize XXXVIII: Best of the Small Presses* and *Uncommon Core: Poems for Learning and Living* (Red Beard Press).

"Night Manual" was chosen by Kimiko Hahn as the winner of the 2013 Michael R. Gutterman Award for Poetry presented by the University of Michigan.

Notes

"The Chinese Farmer Sells His Robots" is inspired by the homemade robots of
Wu Yulu.

"Pop Blasted" makes use of language repurposed from Randy Kennedy's article
"When the Space Age Blasted Off, Pop Culture Followed," which appeared in
the September 25, 2007, issue of *The New York Times*.

My deepest gratitude:

To Edward Haworth Hoeppner, Annie Gilson, Laura Kasischke, A. Van Jordan,
Thomas Lynch, and Keith Taylor, for tending the flame. Your endless reservoirs
of encouragement and faith made this book possible. To the Bear River Writers'
Conference: a true and generous community to which I am grateful for providing
the space, time, and inspiration that led to the genesis of many of these poems
and many yet to come. To the Helen Zell Writers Program at the University of

Michigan and my kind and brilliant peers from the 2014 MFA cohort. To Lauren Clark, Derrick Austen, Marcelo Hernandez Castillo, Andrew Collard, Monica Rico, Jennifer Sperry Steinorth, Ellen Stone, Carrie & Tim Tebeau, Scott Beal, and John Buckley. You're all here in more ways than you know. Sincere apologies to all of you whose names should be written here but aren't.

Final and greatest thanks to Sebastian, Esther Joy, Nora, and Levi, truest wonders, and to Janice, always and for everything—this book is for you.

About the Author

David Hornibrook grew up in the suburbs of Detroit, where he worked for many years as a caregiver and non-profit administrator. His poems have won multiple awards, including a Pushcart Prize. Hornibrook holds an MFA from the Helen Zell Writer's Program at the University of Michigan.